CASE MEMORIAL LIBRARY, ORANGE

3 2159 00125 0279

Withdrawn

P9-CET-200

THE ATHENIANS is a rare reading experience, in a new and exciting form.

Before you is a street in Athens, alive in detail and reality. You stop at an instrument maker's shop, where a lyre is being made by scooping out the insides of a tortoise shell. Nearby a potter's wheel turns. You are part of the crowd at the Panathenaic Stadium where the athletic contests are held. You stand at the entrance to the Parthenon and find it hard to believe this temple was completed in ten years. With a Greek farm boy, you watch as a young slave is sold and you feel his loneliness and fear.

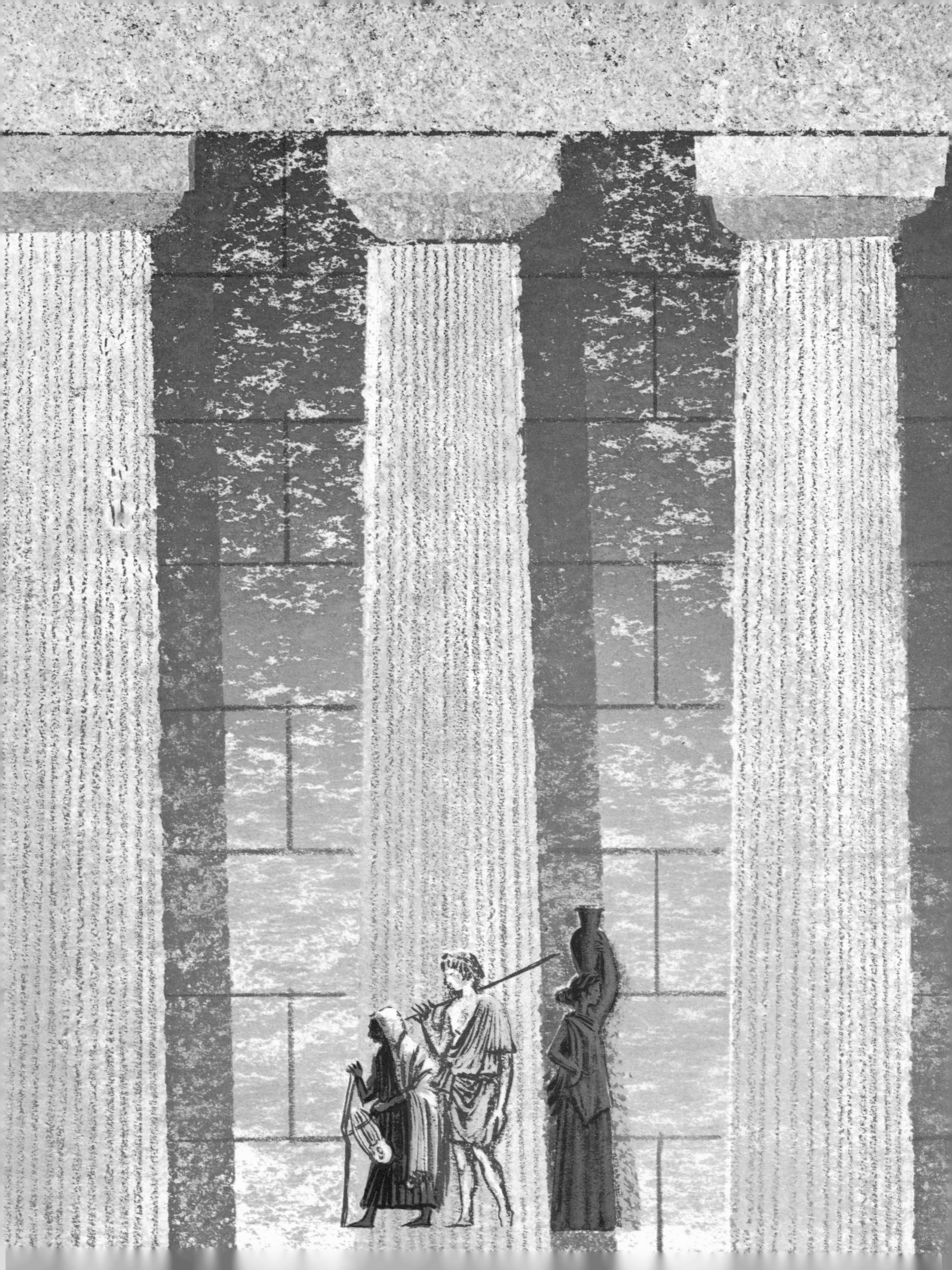

Books in the Life Long Ago Series

The Life Long Ago books are close-up views of ancient civilizations. Everyday life is brilliantly re-created in panoramic, authentic drawings and concise text. Each book is a rare visual experience. Each takes the reader into the reality and excitement of history and provides an extraordinary understanding of a people and their ways.

THE ATHENIANS in the Classical Period

Pictures and Text by LEONARD WEISGARD

The beauty and reality of Athens is before you in the streets of the city as you visit an instrument maker's shop, join the crowds at the Panathenaic Stadium and stand before the Parthenon.

THE CAVE DWELLERS in the Old Stone Age

Pictures and Text by RICHARD M. POWERS

The pictures burst with life and strength. You feel the tense anticipation of the hunters as they gather before the magician in the ritual cave. You know the fear as they face a live mammoth, and realize they must kill or be killed.

THE EGYPTIANS in the Middle Kingdom

Pictures by SHANE MILLER
Text by EDWARD OCHSENSCHLAGER

A fascinating trip through this ancient land where you will visit the lonely Pharaoh of Egypt, walk through the shop-lined streets of Memphis and journey past the great pyramids of Giza.

THE ROMANS in the Days of the Empire

Pictures and Text by SHANE MILLER

The mighty Roman Empire is vividly alive in the strength of these pictures. You take your seat among 45,000 spectators at the Colosseum. You follow a freedman home to his four-story apartment house and you feel the might of the Roman army as they prepare for battle.

0110 UP

©1963 by Leonard Weisgard
All rights reserved.
Library of Congress Catalog Card Number: 63-10176
Manufactured in the United States of America

LIFE LONG AGO

Editorial and Historical Consultant **Edward Ochsenschlager**
ARCHAEOLOGIST AND LECTURER IN CLASSICS

THE ATHENIANS
In the Classical Period

LEONARD WEISGARD

Education Consultant **Rosemary Daly**
LIBRARIAN, ETHICAL CULTURE SCHOOL, NEW YORK

COWARD-McCANN
New York

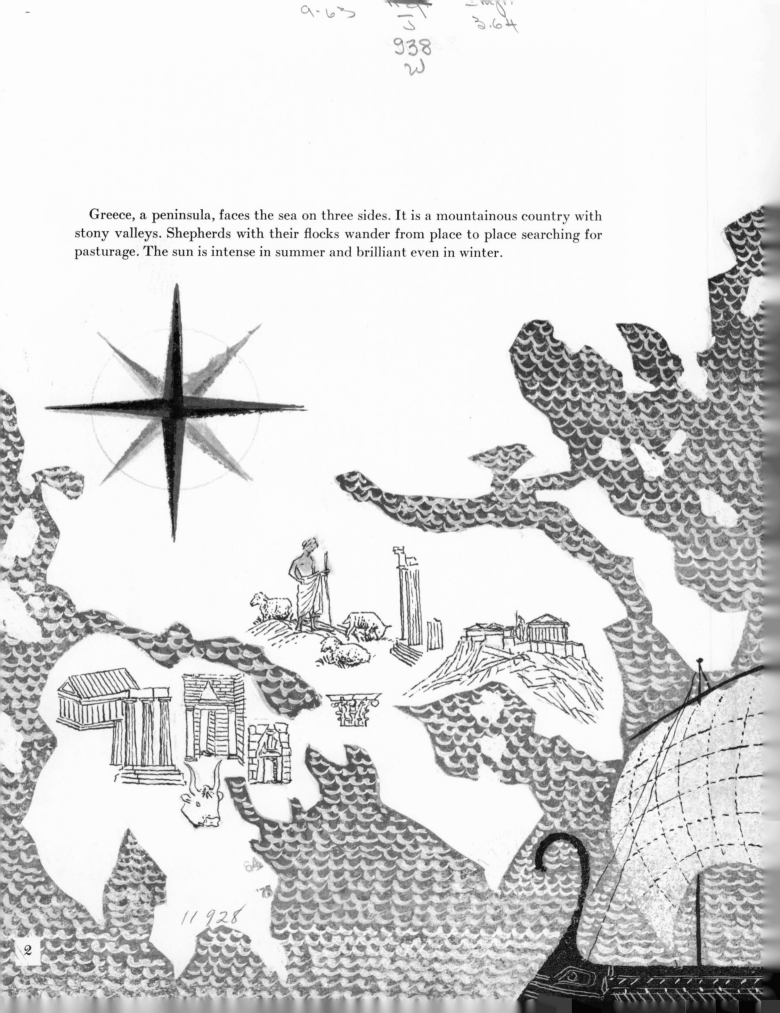

Greece, a peninsula, faces the sea on three sides. It is a mountainous country with stony valleys. Shepherds with their flocks wander from place to place searching for pasturage. The sun is intense in summer and brilliant even in winter.

Timotheus, a Greek boy, worked alongside his father from dawn to dusk. When his father tilled the land, Timotheus often guided the donkey or oxen that pulled the plow.

The Greek farmer owning his own small plot of land produced from his orchards and tilled fields whatever the Grecian earth would bear. With the help of manures and crop rotation, food was produced throughout the year. Irrigation was necessary in much of the Greek countryside. Drawing water for orchards and gardens was hard work for the family.

The farmer's wife was responsible for running the household. She saw to the spinning and carding of wool. She made clothes and prepared the meals. She took charge of the supply of food the farm produced, making it last from harvest to harvest.

At home the farmer's wife educated her boys until they were six years old and ready for school and her girls until they married.

Greek housewives seldom left their homes. They ventured out only for religious services, an occasional visit, or a trip to the market to sell the farm produce.

Hestia was the goddess of the hearth, the deity of the household, worshiped by the entire family.

The light before dawn rose beyond Mount Hymettus. Timotheus was asleep in a sparsely furnished room. A cock crowed and the morning song of birds awakened the boy. This was his day! Today Timotheus would take his honey to the market place in Athens. His father would meet him later for the celebration of the Panathenaic Festival.

Greek farmers had little furniture: a few chairs, couches, tables and one or two chests. Pots, pans and household utensils were either hung on the walls or set about the floor. All the rooms of the farmhouse opened onto the courtyard.

Fruit trees, small vegetable and flower gardens flourished around the farmhouse and courtyard. The farm supplied the household with food. Goats and sheep provided milk. Cheese made from this milk was an important source of food. Chickens provided eggs and meat.

Larger farms produced vegetables, fruits and flowers for sale in the market. Flowers were in demand, for wreaths, festivals and religious services.

Under the towering peaks of Mount Hymettus, bees manufactured a honey famous for its flavor of wild thyme and for its pale color. This was the chief sweetener, used not only for cooking, but as a preservative and as a medicine. Sugar was then unknown and there was a ready market for honey in the ancient world.

Timotheus was not the first on the stony road to the city. Athens drew all kinds of people. Slaves, freedmen, wealthy landowners, were all in the throng before him.

The farmer broke ground for planting with a plow made from a tree trunk, pulled by a yoke of oxen. Wheat and barley, olives and grapes were the main crops. At harvest time, the grain was cut with a sickle and bound in sheaves. It was then dried and spread upon open threshing floors. Cattle driven round and round upon it separated the grain from the straw. When thrown into the air, the heavier grain would settle back to the floor, the lighter chaff would fall to the side.

Oil was processed from the olive. It was the most important agricultural export of Greece. Olives were squeezed in presses. The first pressing yielded a table oil. The Greeks had no butter. Oil from the second pressing was mixed with an alkali into paste and was used as a soap. Because of the scarcity of water, pure oil was often rubbed on the body. The oil and the dust were then scraped off with a strigil. The third pressing supplied oil for lamps. The remainder, skins and all, was used for fuel.

In September the farmer picked his grapes. For ten days they were ripened in the sun, and for five days more were set in the shade. Then the grapes were placed in a wine press. To the music of flutes, the farmer and his helpers danced barefooted upon the grapes. The juice ran off through an outlet at one side of the press, was collected in jars and stored away to ferment. Water was poured over the pressed grape skins and a second stamping produced an inferior wine.

Demeter was the goddess responsible for the crops. She brought greenness and fertility to the Grecian countryside.

In a blaze of brilliant morning sun over the hills, Timotheus saw Athena's spearhead gleam over her city, from the Acropolis.

Athens was the center of the Athenian state, or polis, which included the surrounding country, called Attica.

Although Greek states were small, they influenced deeply the whole economic, religious, moral, educational and cultural life of their people.

The citizens of Athens, those eligible to vote, numbered roughly 20,000 and the polis contained only 1,000 square miles. The total population, including women, children, resident aliens, freedmen and slaves was close to 300,000.

The city of Athens was under the protection of the goddess Athena, the daughter of Zeus, supreme ruler of the gods.

Approaching the city, Timotheus set down his jars of honey and watched a funeral procession leaving Athens.

In Athens, when a man died, the women of the family closed his eyes and mouth and covered his head with a cloth. They washed the body and anointed it. Dressed in finest white clothes, a floral crown upon his head, the body was set upon a couch, face toward the door of the house. In his mouth was an obol, a small coin, should he need money.

A funerary dirge was played by hired mourners. Professional wailers shrieked and beat their breasts while friends and relatives gathered around to say farewell.

The body was carried upon the shoulders of friends to a grave beside the road. Female relatives followed. Relatives brought vases, household goods and other gifts to the grave, hoping the departed would be satisfied with these and not return to claim his property. When the grave was filled, the dead man was called three times by name. Floral wreaths were placed and wine was poured on the soil to slake the departed's thirst. The funeral over, the mourners returned to the dead man's house for the customary funeral banquet. The mourning family had shaved off their hair as a gift for the dead and wore traditional black for thirty days.

Some Greeks believed there was no life at all after death. Others believed in a paradise, or in a shadowy existence in Hades. Though many were uncertain what to believe, Greeks customarily made symbolic preparations for the hereafter.

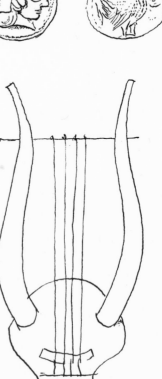

Timotheus was caught up and swept along in the clamorous movement through the Diomean gate to Athens.

Narrow cobbled streets were lined with houses of mud brick over stone rubble foundations. The outer wall of a house shut out the noise and smell of the town. There were usually few rooms within, dimly lit by olive-oil lamps attached to the walls. In the winter, portable stoves provided heat.

Water for the household came from a public fountain, private well, or rainwater cistern. Toilets were built near the street door, flushed with jars of water into the gutter outside.

Nearly every citizen owned his own home. It was against the law for non-citizens to own property. Wealthy Athenians found it a good investment. Many resident aliens and freedmen were well-to-do and could afford a high rent for a good house.

Houses could also be split up into small apartments for the less affluent, with single rooms for the poor. Such a property was managed by a steward who collected the rents and looked after the upkeep of the house.

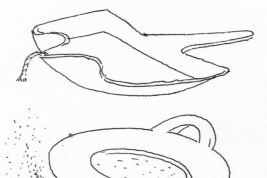

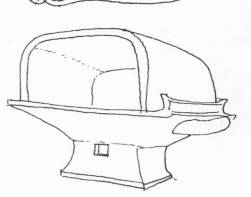

Outside the Bouleuterion, the Greek senate house, where members of the Council met, Timotheus gaped in wonder at the costume of a passing magistrate.

Athens was a democracy. The whole body of citizens participated directly in the government. Every citizen had a seat in the popular Assembly. A citizen could become a candidate for any office and, during his lifetime, almost every citizen held some office at least once.

Government was carried on by the people, the Council and the magistrates. The Assembly was the legislative body of the polis and elected the members of the Council and the magistrates. The magistrates were the administrative body. The Council prepared the programma, a statement of all business which would be submitted in the Assembly to the vote of the people, and also shared with the magistrates the general administration of the state.

A salary was paid by the polis to all in public office. The poor man and his richer neighbor could both afford to neglect his personal affairs to serve the state.

Timotheus rented selling space in the market place. Almost at once a traveling merchant from Corinth purchased his entire supply of honey.

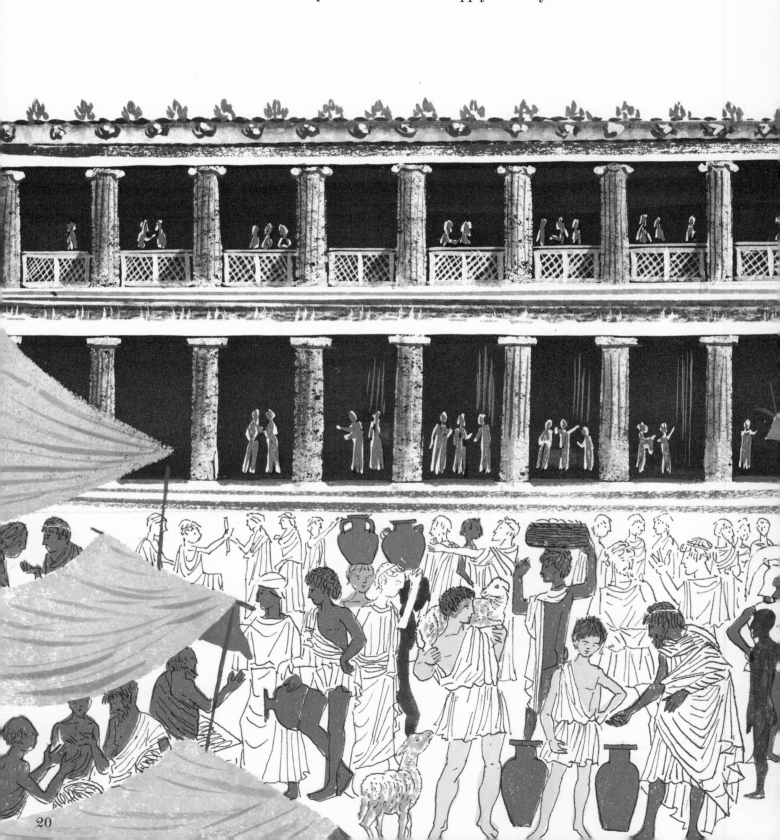

Through the city's gates all streets led to the market place, the Agora. The market place was also the center of Athenian social life. It was crowded with booths, stalls and tables. Among them throngs of people haggled over prices, others cried out the quality of their wares, each adding to the hustle and bustle.

There was a certain order amid the chaos. The selling places were roughly arranged in rows and groups; in each a particular kind of merchandise was sold.

Most of the customers were men. Athenians did not approve of women shoppers, though some of the selling was done by countrywomen. Making a purchase, the man often paid for it with coins he held in his mouth. A slave usually attended his master to carry purchases home.

Clerks of the market inspected weights and measures and prevented adulteration of goods. They kept quarrels over prices from developing into fights. They rented entire sections of the market to rent-farmers, who then rented space to individual sellers at a profit.

Watching the sale of a young slave, Timotheus felt a disturbing sense of the boy's loneliness.

At a market in the Agora slaves were sold every day. Once a month there were special markets when they were sold in greater numbers. Most of them were captured in raids or as prisoners of war. Only a few were Greek. The price varied from about $50 to well over $1,000 depending upon their aptitudes, skill and comeliness. The law drew a sharp distinction between the freeman and the slave, but in practice this was often ignored. In Athens a freeman who struck a slave could be criminally prosecuted. Even the owner's rights were limited by law. If subjected to great cruelty, a slave could take sanctuary in a temple and demand to be sold to another master. It was also against the law for a master to put a slave to death.

Many slaves were content and even happy with their life. However, most slaves lived with the hope and ambition of being free. With money they earned and with patience and time enough, they could purchase liberation.

Wandering away, Timotheus heard the sounds of a lyre being tuned. He looked into a musical instrument maker's shop.

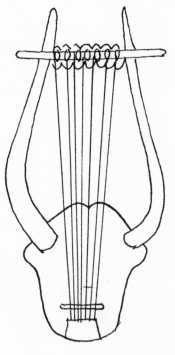

A lyre was made by scooping out the insides of a tortoise shell. Stalks of reed, cut to measure, were fixed in the shell. To close the holes formerly used by the tortoise for his head and legs, a strip of oxhide was stretched around the shell. Horns of wood were attached, to which a top bar was jointed. On the underside of the shell, a bridge was set. Seven strings of sheep gut were fastened to a tailpiece, stretched across the bridge, wound around the bar, pulled as tight as need be and tied.

The cithara was made in the same manner, but with a wooden body. A larger sounding board gave it a fuller tone.

Instrument making was a thriving business in Athens. Bonds of fellowship were strong among the instrument makers as in all the crafts. Every craft had its own association for social and religious purposes. The members met together to discuss their work and pay honor to the god, the founder, or a hero associated with their craft.

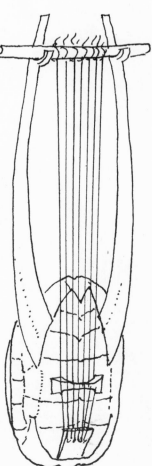

Through an open doorway, Timotheus saw a potter's wheel turning.

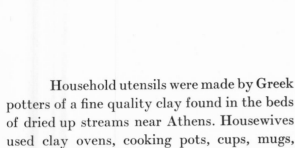

Household utensils were made by Greek potters of a fine quality clay found in the beds of dried up streams near Athens. Housewives used clay ovens, cooking pots, cups, mugs, amphoras and vases of different shapes and sizes.

Such utensils were formed on the potter's wheel, turned by an apprentice. Amphoras, commercial containers made of clay and decorated vases were also exported in trade to various parts of the ancient world.

A vase, when formed on the wheel and partly dried, had the excess clay removed with a knife, and was then ready for decorating. Figures or a design were sketched on with a charcoal stick. Applied with a brush, a broad band of black glaze outlined the decoration on the vase, and relief lines were added. The background was filled in with a black glaze. Sometimes reds of different intensities, white and gold leaf were added. The vase was polished with a soft cloth and then fired in a kiln. Vase decorations represented the great variety and richness of life in Greece.

The Greek potter took great pride in everything he made, but especially in the pottery used for ceremonial rituals. At the Panathenaic Festival large amphoras were given as prizes for athletic contests. On one side of the amphora was depicted the figure of Athena with the inscription, *I am from the Games of Athens*. On the other a painting showed the contest for which the vase was a prize.

27

The crowds parted to make way for a limping merchant. Timotheus watched him approach the workshop of a physician.

Hippocrates is often given credit for the origin of scientific medicine. Long before he lived, however, the Greeks had professional physicians. Only a little was known of anatomy and even less of how certain parts of the body worked.

Physicians were generally scientific. They did not believe that disease was caused by the gods or spirits. They recognized and acknowledged the natural basis of disease and the evidence of its causes. From early times careful observations of symptoms probably played a considerable part in their clinical practice.

Offices or workshops served as hospitals, where pupils acted as nurses. A physician seldom performed surgery. This work was usually entrusted to wandering "specialists," who went their way once the operation was completed. In days when surgery often proved fatal, it was better to be away from irate relatives in the event the patient died.

Physicians belonged to guilds into which novices were solemnly initiated. The novices were urged to adopt high standards of honor, integrity, secrecy, obedience to the laws, and loyalty to the interests of their patients.

Asclepius was the god of medicine.

A young voice dramatically reciting Homer brought Timotheus to a stop in front of a school.

At the age of six a boy was placed under the care of a trusted slave, who taught him manners and bearing becoming an Athenian. One duty of the slave was to attend the boy to and from school.

There were no public schools in Athens. All parents, however, were expected to see that their sons were properly educated. They sent their boys to private schools, paying fees to professional teachers.

In the morning, students learned to read and write. They scratched letters with a stylus on the wax-covered surface of a wooden tablet. One end of the stylus was pointed for writing. The other end was flat, used to smooth the wax when a mistake was made.

Literature and music were important studies but the development of character was education's primary aim. The goal of the Greek school was to nurture moral, mental and physical perfection in boys who would grow to be citizens fit to render service to Athens.

Timotheus' attention was drawn by cheers and shouts to the courtyard of the school.

The second part of the school day was devoted to exercise in the courtyard. The palaestra, gymnasium, was a low building with an open central courtyard. Within were rooms for undressing. The ideal palaestra had a stream running alongside the court. Otherwise, provisions for washing were inside.

Boys participated in athletics, naked, out of doors, taking full advantage of the heat of the sun. Boys trained in running, the broad jump, the high jump, and the throwing of weights and spears. Their hands bound with leather thongs, they also learned to box.

Athletes anointed themselves with olive oil, and wrestlers sprinkled themselves with fine sand to allow their opponents a better grip. The exercises over, oil, dust and sweat were scraped off with a strigil, and the boys enjoyed a cold swim.

After the age of sixteen, these exercises became the most important part of a boy's education.

As Timotheus left the school a chariot stopped at a house nearby. Wedding guests tossed a golden shower of grain over the bride and groom. Someone handed Timotheus a sweetmeat.

Parents or professional matchmakers arranged a marriage. The wife was usually much younger than the husband. Men about the age of thirty married girls as young as sixteen. The betrothal took place in the girl's house.

At the wedding feast given by the bride's father, a sacrifice was made to the household gods. On one side of the room sat the women, the men on the other. They ate the wedding cake made of pounded grain, sesame and honey, and drank much wine.

Then the groom took the veiled bride to their home in a chariot. His best friend drove the horses. A crowd of revelers, musicians and the girl's mother followed along.

Showered with grain, fruits and sweetmeats, they passed through the door. The groom carried the bride over the threshold. With religious ceremony, the groom's parents received the girl into the family. Then the couple were ushered into the bridal chamber by the guests.

Once inside, the bride and groom ate a quince together, as prescribed by law. This symbolized that their life together would have bitter as well as happy moments. In final tribute to the bride and groom, the wedding guests sang an epithalamium, a marriage chamber song.

Timotheus made his way to the home of his father's guest-friend. Here he was to meet his father.

Such cause for joy and celebration. An olive branch hung on the door. Know all who enter here, a son has been born!

Guest-friendships were customary among the Greeks. The rights and duties of such relationships were inherited. Each man was given the full hospitality of the other whenever he found himself near his friend's home. They might live in different parts of the polis, different parts of Greece, or even different parts of the world beyond Greece.

When a Greek mother gave birth, a midwife or sometimes a slave assisted her. After birth, to gain strength from the earth and buried ancestors, the baby was laid on the ground. The father picked up the baby to show that he recognized and accepted the child as his own. The infant was dressed and placed in a basket. On the front door of the house, the father hung an olive branch. A woolen ribbon would be hung if the baby were a girl.

The first formal ceremony took place on about the fifth day. For this religious ceremony, the mother and attendants were purified by ritual bathing and the house by ritual sweeping. Running naked about the hearth the father held the child in his arms. This, it was believed, would bring the child strength to walk soon and run fast.

On about the tenth day, the father gave a banquet. Friends and relatives were invited and all brought gifts for the baby.

When a man's guests arrived, slaves removed the guests' sandals and washed their feet. They brought tables and couches for them, and poured water over their hands. Dinner was served in the andron or dining room.

If a man had no guests, his wife might dine with him, seated in a chair while he reclined at the table; otherwise the women and children had their meal apart. It was considered barbarous to eat alone.

For the banquet to commemorate the birth of a child, as on most special occasions, a professional male cook was hired. As part of the celebration a sacrifice was made to the gods and the child was named.

For Greek parents, the lack of male children was a bitter thing. There would be no son to carry on the family religion of the hearth. The parents would be denied the burial due them. And in the years to come who would make the accustomed sacrifices at their graves? It was almost as great a calamity to the polis, which depended on a strong body of male citizens for protection against its enemies.

That night, after dining, Timotheus, beside his father, shared the wonder of a singer and his lyre, reciting selections from Euripides. For Timotheus, a farm boy who had never been to the Greek theatre, the singer's recital gave life to a world he had only imagined.

The theatre in Athens was not primarily a place of amusement. Greek drama was religious in character, and deeply moving to the audience. Dramatic works were written for a single performance only and performed in competition with the works of other playwrights. The actor wore a mask fitted with a resonant mouthpiece of brass, and a wig to indicate the character of the part he played. In tragedy actors wore shoes with high soles to give them the added dignity of height.

Sponsoring plays was one of the chief duties of the richer citizens. The man who undertook this duty, the choragus, paid for the training of the chorus, provided costumes and other necessities. People attending the drama had to pay for their seats. But drama was considered so important that if a citizen were too poor, the polis would pay his price of admission.

Tragedy consisted of dramatic poetry, serious in purpose, set to appropriate music and performed with great precision of movement and gesture. Its subject matter was chosen from mythology and everyone in the audience knew the story in advance. The audience was therefore more interested in the author's interpretation than in the plot.

Comedy was essentially musical, for the words were often recited to music. The author was permitted great freedom of expression. He mercilessly satirized events, issues and well-known people of his time.

In the four days ahead, Timotheus and his father would participate in the glories of the Panathenaic festival. These days would be crowded with events.

To the Odeum or music hall thronged not only Athenians but many other Grecians who had come great distances to be a part of the festival.

The building, roofed with the yards and masts of ships captured from the Persians, stood next to the theatre.

Here were held various kinds of musical contests. The most popular was singing to the accompaniment of the lyre. Men also competed with each other reciting Homeric poems, accompanying themselves on a lyre or cithara.

Athletic contests were held in the Panathenaic stadium which was about 850 feet long and stood in a narrow valley south and a little east of the Acropolis. Spectators sat on the slopes.

The contests included three kinds of foot races: the quarter-mile race, the long race of two to three miles, and races with the contestants carrying war shields. Wrestling took place on ground specially prepared to break falls and give the athletes a foothold. Boxing and Pankration events went on until one of the contestants admitted defeat. In the latter, any kind of fighting was permitted. Only eye-gouging and biting were barred.

Another contest, the pentathlon, was designed to test the all-round athlete. It consisted of five events: the foot race, the long jump, throwing the javelin, throwing the discus and wrestling. Only those who gained a certain number of points in the first four were allowed to enter the wrestling. The winner must have not only strength but also agility, grace and skill. The youth who excelled in all sports was truly a man most respected and admired by the Greeks.

On the last day of the festivities, boat racing was held at the Peiraieus. All Athenians, Timotheus and his father among them, gathered to watch.

As athletic contests on land developed the strength and endurance of men for battle, so the boat races developed their skill and co-ordination for war at sea.

The Peiraieus was the seaport of Athens and joined to it by two long parallel walls. Athens was the center of a great naval empire with the largest navy in the Greek world. The trireme was the basis of her fleet, a large ship with three banks of oars.

Naval tactics of the time used the ship as a kind of missile, rowing or sailing it into the enemy's vessel and quickly withdrawing it by means of counter rowing. Another tactic was launching the ship against the enemy as if intending to ram him. Then at the last moment the ship would swerve and run close alongside. The bulk of the trireme would break off the enemy's oars and the marines would rake his deck with arrows. The disabled enemy might then be rammed and sunk at will. In order to be totally effective, such tactics must be carried out at high speed.

The crew of each trireme was made up of 170 rowers, eight officers and ten marines. The sailors were almost all Athenian citizens. Though citizens might have special privileges, they also bore the sole responsibility for the defense of the country.

On the Acropolis, at the entrance to the sacred precinct, the Propylaea, Timotheus stands with his father. Beyond its five gates is the Parthenon, the Erechtheum and the great altar of Zeus and Athena, where the Panathenaic procession will end.

To the Greeks the Parthenon, Athena's temple, was almost miraculous. It had been built in ten years, a fact in itself hard to believe. Even less understandably, beyond the actual size of the Parthenon, the illusion was one greater than reality.

Workmen first quarried huge blocks, then built a road from the quarry at Mount Pentelicus to the temple site. Wagons of tremendous strength had to be constructed to bear great loads. Thirty to forty pairs of oxen were required to drag each block, and in a full day's work could move it only ten miles.

The workmen moved, fitted, finished and sometimes raised these blocks to great heights on the building site, without the help of cranes. The columns of the Parthenon were over thirty-four feet high.

Under the direction of Phidias, the Parthenon was decorated with sculpture. As was customary, sections of the decorations were put in charge of individual contractors. But under the influence of this great master, all the many parts came together to produce a wondrous unity and harmony.

Inside, Phidias created a statue of Athena, seven times life size. Her flesh was made of ivory and her dress and decorations were of gold.

Chosen Athenian women have carefully woven a new peplos, a robe for the statue of Athena Polias in the Erechtheum. On the mast of a ship pulled along on rollers the peplos is carried to the altar of Zeus and Athena, northeast of the Parthenon.

Toward the altar moves a vast procession. Magistrates of the city and citizens selected for their lineage, dignity and physical perfection, prize-winning athletes, soldiers in full armor, unmarried girls from the oldest and noblest families, sacred delegations from allied states, all move on. Parade marshals are keeping proper order. Behind the ship come maidens with sacrificial dishes, grain, torches and implements such as knives and blunt stunning instruments. Cattle and sheep with gilded horns and wearing garlands follow. Then come attendants and musicians. Then chariots, each with a marshal, warrior and charioteer, and finally groups of knights on horseback — men from the middle class who can afford a horse and full armor.

As the procession passes, crowds of people who have come to watch flood into the sacred precinct, to take part in the sacrifice.

49

When the presentation of the peplos is completed, the sacrificial victims are led to the altar. The animals come willingly, nodding their heads. This is a good omen. The officiating priests and priestesses, wearing garlands like those of the victims, sanctify a large dish of water by plunging a torch taken from the altar into it. The altar and all present are sprinkled with this sacred water.

In the silence following come the prayers of the chief priestess, standing with her hands raised, palms upward toward Olympia, where Athena dwells. Sacred barley is sprinkled on and around the victims. The priests and priestesses cut a bit of hair from each animal and throw it into the fire. The animals are stunned with a club, their throats are cut and the blood is collected in vessels, poured on the altar. The heads of the dying beasts are kept turned upward toward Olympia. Then the beasts are skinned and cut up. The tails, fat, joints and thighbones are burned on the altars for the goddess. The rest is cooked on spits and distributed to the people.

Throughout the ceremonies the attending crowd cry aloud to Athena in prayer.

At the hour when shadows lengthen, Timotheus and his father are returning home. Both are silent. Within the boy is boundless wonderment.

THE OLYMPIAN GODS

ZEUS (zus)
— the supreme god. He was the god of the sky, heavenly phenomena (lightning, thunder, rain), the protector of hospitality, and of all Greece. Usually represented with the thunderbolt in right hand, scepter in left hand, eagle at his feet.

HERA (hē′ra)
— the sister and wife of Zeus. She was the queen of the gods and the patron divinity of marriage and maternity. Usually holding a scepter surmounted by a cuckoo and a pomegranate. The peacock was sacred to her.

HESTIA (hes′ti·a)
— the sister of Zeus. She was the goddess of the hearth and protectress of the house, the family, and the city. Seldom represented.

POSEIDON (po·si′don)
— the brother of Zeus. He was the god of earthquakes, the sea, and horses. Generally represented with the trident.

DEMETER (de·mē′ter)
— the sister of Zeus. She was the goddess of the earth, grain, and agriculture. Usually shown crowned with a ribbon, in her hands ears of corn or a torch.

HEPHAESTUS (he·fēs′tus)
— the son of Zeus and Hera. He was the god of fire, the patron god of mechanical arts (toolmakers, armorers, potters, etc.), the divine blacksmith who forged the armor of gods and heroes. Generally shown with conical headgear, in his hands a hammer, tongs, bellows.

ARES (a′rēz)
— the son of Zeus and Hera. He was the god of offensive war. Most often represented with spear and war helmet.

ATHENA
— the daughter of Zeus, born from his head. She was the goddess of wisdom, defensive war, the arts of peace; and the patron deity of Athens. Usually represented with the aegis (a short goatskin cloak with zigzag edges), war helmet, spear and shield.

APHRODITE (af·ro·di′te)
— the daughter of Zeus and Dione. She was the goddess of love, beauty, and fertility. Usually represented rising from the foam of the waves, at her bath, or with her winged son, Eros.

APOLLO
— the son of Zeus and Leto. He was the god of the sun, archery, music, medicine, prophecy, the protector of flocks, and the patron divinity of young men. Generally represented with either the lyre, the bow and quiver, or the shepherd's crook.

ARTEMIS (ar′te·mis)
— the twin sister of Apollo. She was the goddess of the moon, wild animals, hunting, the patron goddess of maidens and of childbirth. Most often shown carrying a bow and quiver, and accompanied by a dog or doe.

HERMES (hur′mēz)
— the son of Zeus and Maia. He was the god of travelers, commerce, profit, cunning and thieves. He also conducted the souls of the dead to the underworld and was the messenger of the gods. Generally represented with a round winged hat, winged sandals, and a winged staff entwined with serpents.

OTHER GREEK GODS

— the brother of Zeus. Ruler of the underworld and the souls of the dead. Seldom represented. The cypress was sacred to him.

HADES

HADES was also the name given to the abode of the dead. When THANATOS (Death), the son of night and the brother of HYPNOS (Sleep), dispatched a human being with his fatal sword, and when that human was properly buried, the soul went on a journey guided by Hermes. Charon was the ferryman who rowed souls across the river Styx. At the entrance to Hades stood the monstrous three-headed watchdog, Cerberus. Judgment on the soul was pronounced by Hades and his three assessors: Aeacus, Minos, and Rhadamanthys, and the soul was assigned to Tartarus, the place of punishment, or the Elysian Fields, the abode of the blessed. Famous mortals who the Greeks thought had journeyed to the underworld and managed to return were Heracles, Theseus, Orpheus, Odysseus and Aeneas.

PERSEPHONE (per·sĕf′ō·nĕ)

— the daughter of Zeus and Demeter. Queen of the underworld and wife of Hades. She was abducted by Hades. Grief-stricken, Demeter searched the world for her. Zeus ordered her restored to her mother. But she had eaten in Hades, and was required to return there a part of each year. When Persephone was with her mother, Demeter was happy and tended to her duties. This was spring and summer. When Persephone was in Hades, Demeter grieved and neglected the earth. This was fall and winter. Usually represented with the bat and pomegranate.

DIONYSUS (dī′o·nī′sŭs)

— the son of Zeus and Semele. He was the god of wine, vegetation, and pleasure. Hera made him insane and he wandered about the world followed by centaurs, satyrs, and maenads. Generally shown crowned with vine leaves and bunches of grapes, in one hand a wine cup or bunches of grapes.

MUSES

— the nine daughters of Zeus and Mnemosyne (Memory). Each goddess protected a different sphere of literature, fine arts, and science: CLIO, history; EUTERPE, lyric poetry; THALIA, comedy; MELPOMENE, tragedy; TERPSICHORE, lyric poetry and the dance; ERATO, love poetry; POLYHYMNIA, heroic hymns and the art of mime; URANIA, astronomy; CALLIOPE, epic poetry and eloquence.

MOERAE (mē′rē) **or FATES**

— the three daughters of night. They determined the destiny of human beings. CLOTHO, the spinner, spun the thread of life. LACHESIS drew the thread out. When man was destined to die, ATROPOS cut the thread.

NEMESIS (nĕm′ĕ·sĭs)

— a goddess who represented the anger of the gods. She punished human beings who were insolent, arrogant or excessively proud.

EUMENIDES (ū·mĕn′ĭ·dēz)
or ERINYES (ĕ·rĭn′ĭ·ēz)
or FURIES

— three goddesses of vengeance, ALECTO, TISIPHONE, and MEGAERA. They were armed with whips and torches, their hair bristling with serpents. They punished those who committed serious crimes by pursuing them and driving them insane.

ASCLEPIUS (ăs·klē′pĭ·ŭs)

— the son of Apollo. He was transformed from a mortal into a god and became the god of medicine. Generally shown with the snake.

HYGEA (hī·jē′ă)

— the daughter of Asclepius. The goddess of health.

A CHRONOLOGY OF THE FIFTH CENTURY

490 B.C. The Athenian General Miltiades defeated the overwhelming forces of Darius, King of Persia, on the plain of Marathon.

480 B.C. Xerxes, son of Darius, gathered all the available strength of the Persian Empire and invaded Greece. At the Pass of Thermopylae tens of thousands of Persians were held in check for three days by Leonidas, King of Sparta, and 300 men. Then the Persians swept on, occupied and destroyed Athens. The Greek fleet remained intact, however, and under the direction of the Athenian admiral, Themistocles, decoyed the more numerous Persian navy into the narrow straits of Salamis and crushingly defeated them.

479 B.C. The Greek victories at Plataea and Mycale completed the liberation of Greece from the Persians and thereby secured a European independence of Asia.

477 B.C. The Delian League, an offensive and defensive alliance of Greek city-states against Persia, was formed with Athens as the dominant partner.

ca. 460—429 B.C. Pericles was the most influential man at Athens. He represented the highest ideals of his age.

459 B.C. Athens sent naval support to aid an insurrection against the Persian king in Egypt.

456 B.C. Athens reached the height of her power on land.

453 B.C. The Athenian naval expedition to Egypt was destroyed.

448 B.C. The Delian League was changed into an Athenian empire.

431 B.C. The growing power of Athens, which threatened her rival, Sparta, led to the outbreak of the Peloponnesian War.

430 B.C. A serious plague broke out in Athens, killing a third of the population.

429 B.C. The death of Pericles.

421 B.C. The Peace of Nicias began. The terms of peace were kept by neither side, but the Athenians and Spartans refrained from invading each other's territory for nearly seven years.

415–413 B.C. An Athenian expedition was sent against Syracuse in Sicily. The Athenian forces were utterly defeated.

404 B.C. The fall of Athens.

SOME FAMOUS FIFTH-CENTURY GREEKS AT ATHENS

AESCHYLUS (524/5–456 B.C.) — a dramatist. Seven of his tragedies have survived.

ALCAMENES (ca. 460–400 B.C.) — a sculptor who worked in the Hephaesteum, a temple of Hephaestus and Athena near the Agora, and the temple of Ares in Athens.

ARISTOPHANES (ca. 450–ca. 385 B.C.) — the earliest writer of comedy whose works are preserved. Eleven of his plays exist today.

CALLICRATES — associated with Ictinus and Phidias in the building of the Parthenon, and designer of the temple of Athena Nike.

CALLIMACHUS — a Greek sculptor. He is credited with being the creator of the Corinthian capital in architecture.

EURIPIDES (ca. 485–ca. 406 B.C.) — a dramatist. Seventeen or eighteen of his tragedies exist today.

HERODOTUS (ca. 484–ca. 425 B.C.) — the father of History, who began writing his monumental work, *The Histories,* in Athens ca. 447 B.C.

HIPPODAMUS — an architect who designed cities and introduced the grid method of laying out streets into European Greece. He remodeled Piraeus.

ICTINUS (fl. after 450 B.C.) — an architect. His most famous work is the Parthenon, in which he was assisted by Callicrates and Phidias.

MICON — a famous Athenian painter and sculptor.

MNESICLES — an architect. He was the designer of the Propylaea and perhaps of the Erechtheum.

PHIDIAS (ca. 490–ca. 417 B.C.) — the most famous sculptor of fifth-century Athens. He designed the marble sculptures of the Parthenon and the thirty-foot bronze statue of Athena which stood on the Acropolis just inside the Propylaea. He was also responsible for the statue of Athena which stood within the Parthenon. This statue was made of wood, ivory and gold, and was seven times life size.

PINDAR (518–438 B.C.) — a lyric poet who was educated at Athens. Some of his odes, commemorating athletic victors at the Olympic, Pythian, Nemean, and Isthmian games, are all of his work which has survived intact.

PLATO (ca. 429–347 B.C.) — a philosopher. He taught men to think through a new literary form which he invented — the dialogue.

POLYGNOTUS (fl. ca. 475–447 B.C.) — the most famous Greek painter of the fifth century.

SOCRATES (469–399 B.C.) — by far the most important thinker of his time. He has had great influence on all subsequent thought.

SOPHOCLES (ca. 496–406 B.C.) — a dramatist. Seven of his tragedies have survived.

THUCYDIDES (ca. 460–400 B.C.) — an historian. He is the author of the (incomplete) *History of the Peloponnesian War.*

XENOPHON (ca. 430–ca. 354 B.C.) — he wrote on a variety of subjects. His best known work is the *Anabasis,* an account of an expedition, under the Persian Cyrus the Younger, of the Greek mercenaries and of their subsequent adventures.

FOR FURTHER READING

Davis, William Stearns, *A Day in Old Athens.* Allyn and Bacon, 1914

A visit to Athens in 360 B.C. with sidelights on schools, houses, sports, religion, costumes and customs

Fawcett, Raymond, ed., *How Did They Live? Greece;* photographs by Robert Benchley. Boston, 1953

Simple text with photographs of arts and artifacts and some reconstruction gives a lively idea of the early Greeks

Grant, Michael, and Pottinger, Don, author-artists, *Greeks.* Nelson, London, 1958

A thoughtful and very well executed book with numerous illustrations

Mills, Dorothy, *The Book of the Ancient Greeks.* Putnam, 1925

An introduction to the history of Greek civilization

Quennell, Marjorie, and Quennell, C. H. B., *Everyday Things in Ancient Greece;* rev. by Kathleen Freeman. Putnam, 1954

Practical information on clothing, shelter, religion and other aspects of life. Not up-to-date, but contains good bibliography of books that are.

Robinson, Charles Alexander, *The First Book of Ancient Greece;* illus. by Lili Rethi. Watts, 1960

Concentrates on the Athens of Pericles, but gives a brief account of earlier and later Greek history

Snedeker, Caroline Dale, *Theras and His Town.* Doubleday, 1961 ed.

A schoolboy's adventures in the Greece of Pericles

Taylor, Duncan, *Ancient Greece.* Roy, 1958

A concentrated and lively presentation of Greeks from mythological times to the death of Alexander

INDEX

This is a partially annotated Index. Where no annotation occurs, the text is fully explanatory. Italics have been used for Latin and Greek words. Italic numerals designate page references to pictures.

Acropolis (ă.krŏp′ō.lĭs) [Means citadel. It is a huge rock about 500 feet above sea level and 190 feet above the highest part of the town. On it were the principle temples of Athens, including the temple of the Wingless Victory, the precinct of *Artemis of Brauronia*, the *Athena Promachos*, the *Erectheion*, which contains the ancient wooden statue, the *Athena Polias* or city warden in whose honor the Panathenaic Festival was held, and the *Parthenon*], *13*, 43, *53*

Agora, see Market place

Amphora(s) [jar with egg-shaped body, long narrow neck, and two handles], *26*, *26*, *27*, *27*, *33*

    Panathenaic, *27*, *27*

Andron (ăn′drŏn) [dining room], *38*, 39

Asclepius [son of *Apollo* and *Coronis*], *29*, *29*

Assembly [*Ecclesia*], 19

Athena [Goddess of wisdom, daughter of *Zeus*, patron of Athens], *12*, 13, *13*, *46*, 47, *50*, 51; *see also* Panathenaic Festival

Athens (*Athenae*) [chief city of *Attica*], 6, 8, 31, 44

Athletics, *32*, 33, *33*, 43, *43*

Attica [the region of ancient Greece that surrounded Athens. Athenians believed it had been formed as a state by *Theseus*], 13; *see also* Panathenaic Festival

Barley, 9, 51

Bees, 7

Betrothal [formal ceremony before witnesses necessary to render the following marriage legal], 35

Birth

    banquet, 37, 39

    ceremonies, 37, *37*

    customs, 36, *36*, 37, 39

    religious rituals, 37, *37*

Boat races, 44, *44*, 45, *45*

Bouleuterion (boo′lū.tē′rĭ.ŏn) [the Council House, one of the main civic buildings, fronting the western side of the *Agora*], 18, *18*, *19*

Boxing, *32*, 33, 43; *see also Pankration*

Carding [cleaning and disentangling fibers before spinning], 5, *5*

Chariot, *12*, 34, *35*

Cheese, 7

Chickens, 7, *7*

Children

    female, 5, *5*, *11*, 35

    male, 5, *5*, *10*, 30, *30*, 31, *31*, *32*, 33, *33*, 39, *39*

Choragus (kō.rā′gŭs) [originally, leader of the chorus], 41

Cithara, *24*, *25*, *25*, *30*, 43

Citizens [Both parents had to be free Athenian citizens for a person to claim citizenship. Children of such were registered at birth in the City records books], 13, 17, 19, 31, 45, *48*, *49*

Clerks, 21

Comedy, 41

Costume [There were only two essential garments in Greek dress — the *chiton* (kī′tŏn) and the *himation* (hĭ.măt′ĭ.ŏn), worn both by men and women. The *chiton* was an oblong woolen garment large enough to wrap around the body closely; one side was fastened with a decorative pin, the other had a slit for the arm; a girdle around the waist adapted the length and formed a bloused top. Men could go out on the street in this garment alone — workmen and slaves wore nothing else. The second garment, the *himation*, was an oblong woolen shawl wrapped tightly around the body and held in place with the hand — no fastenings were ever used. This was worn outdoors only. Women always wore the *himation* in public; men wore it for formal occasions. There was a third garment sometimes used by men called *chlamys* (klă′mĭs), a short, circular mantle favored by travelers, young active men, or men out in bad weather. Sandals were simple leather soles with thongs which could be colored, decorated, or jewel-encrusted], *4*, *5*, 8, 9, *10*, *11*, *12*, *14*, *16*, *17*, 18, *18*, *19*, *20*, *21*, 41, *41*

Council [500 men, fifty from each of the ten Athenian tribes], 19

Courtyard, *32*, *32*, 33, *33*

Crafts, 25

Crop rotation, 3

Death, ceremonies and customs, 14, *14*, 15, *15*

Demeter [sister of *Zeus*, mother of *Persephone*], 11, 15

Democracy, 18

Diomean Gate [one of the many gates leading to the center of the city], 16, *16*

Dionysus [one of the sons of *Zeus*], 15

Dirge [a musical composition expressing grief], *14*, 15

Drama, 40, 41

Education, 5, 30; *see also* School

Epithalamium, 35

Farmhouse [built of sun-dried brick covered with plaster; beaten earth floors; one large room

piety and thrown into prison where he died in 432 B.C., the year in which the *Parthenon* was completed], 47

Physicians, 28, *28*, 29

Plow, 3, *3*, 9

Polis (po'lis), 13, 19

Potters, 26, *26*, 27

Programma (prŏ.grăm'ă), 19

Propylaea (prŏp'ĭlē'ă) [The Ceremonial Gateway was a tremendous marble building the whole western end of the *Acropolis*. It was designed by *Mnesicles* and was built 437 to 432 B.C. The central portion was a double porch with columns 30 feet high], 46, *46*

Quince, 35; *see also* Fruit trees

Rents [About 8% of the value of the house constituted the legal yearly rent. Houses ranged in value from about $100 to $1,800], 17

Resident aliens *(metics)*, 13, 17; *see also* Freedmen

Sacred Precinct [the area of the *Acropolis* between the *Propylaea* and the *Parthenon*], 46, 48, *50, 51*

Sacrifice, 48, *50*, 51, *51*

Sailors, 45

Salary [3 *obol* fee for attendance (9¢)], 19

School, 30, *30*, 31, *31*, 32, *32*, 33, *33*

Scythians [public police force], *21, 22, 23; see also* Slaves

Sheep, *2, 4*, 7, *7*, 9, *20*, 49

Ship(s), *2, 3*, 43, *44*, 45, *45*, 48, *48*

Slave(s) [There were two general classes of slaves. Those privately owned served as domestic servants, pedagogues, factory workers, shop keepers, dock hands, sailors, miners, farm hands, and were kept even by men of moderate means, who often bought them in the *Agora*. Those owned by the city of Athens known as *Demosioi* served as treasury clerks, public executioners and torturers, coin makers at the Mint, and the public police force or *Scythians* numbering 1,200 under military discipline and always at the disposal of the magistrates], 8, *8*, 9, 13, *20, 21, 22, 22, 23, 30*, 31, 37, *37*

Soap, 9

Spinning [turning fibrous material into thread], 5

Stoves, 17, *17*

Strigil, 33, *33*

Stylus, 31, *31*

Sugar, 7

Surgery, 29

Tablet, 31, *31*

Teacher, *30*, 31

Theatre, 40, 41, *41*

Toilets, 17

Tragedy, 41, *41*

Trireme, *44*, 45, *45*

Vases, *4, 5*, 7, *8, 9, 10, 11, 15, 16, 17, 18, 20, 21, 26, 27, 27, 37, 38, 39*

Vegetables, 7

Water, *4*, 5, 17, *17; see also* Irrigation

Wedding
   costume, bride [consisted of a saffron *chiton* and a *himation* of silvery tissue draped over the head and body, white sandals embroidered with jewels, jewelry on fingers, neck and ears, and a wreath of roses in her hair], *34*

   costume, groom [colorful, perhaps a yellow-bordered white *chiton*, a blue *himation*, violet-thonged sandals, and a wreath of myrtle and violets on his head], *34*

   customs, 34, *34*, 35

   feast, 35

   guests, 34, *34*

Wheat, 9

Wig(s), 41, *41*

Wine, *10*, 11, *11*, 15, 35

Wine press, 10, *10*

Women, *4*, 5, *5*, 8, 9, *11*, 14, *14*, 21, *34*, 37, *37, 38, 39, 39*, 48, *49*

Wrestling, 33, *33*, *43*

Zeus, 13

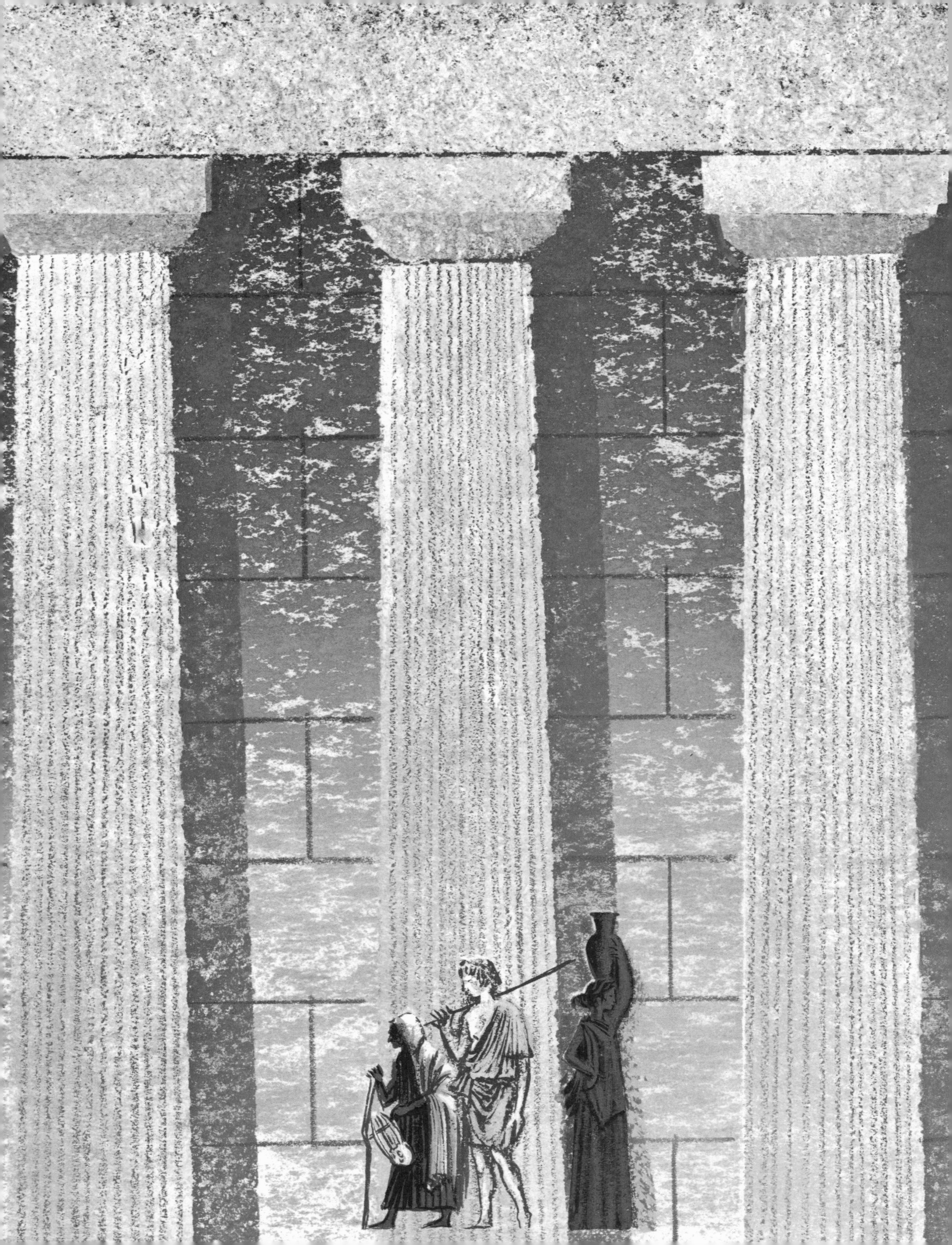